Your #1 Brand is YOU!

[*How to Be Irresistibly Employable*]

by

LeTicia Lee

Your #1 Brand is YOU!

[*How to Be Irresistibly Employable*]

SoRichIam.com

Published via LuLu Press Press, Inc.
860 Aviation Parkway, Suite 300
Morrisville, NC 27560

Letters to the Author can be sent to:

Attn: LeTicia Lee
P.O. Box 20711
Rochester, New York 14602
USA

ISBN 978-1300843849

TABLE OF CONTENTS

In an age when so many seek their self-worth in the name brand clothes, purses, shoes they wear, the cars they drive and other products they own, discover the one brand that can make you the president of a nation, a celebrity, a high profile corporate executive, or president and CEO of a major brand. In fact, you are already the President and CEO of a major brand. Don't believe me?

That major brand is you! It's as unique as your fingerprint. How well are you managing the brand of Y-O-U?

There are no shortcuts to a successful life. But if you put in the initial work, you will create the habit of checking in with yourself and your Creator. You can manifest the best life you never could have planned if you were unaware of what we're about to share in this book.

Get a good journal or notebook. Complete the exercises along the way.

Be patient. This book is designed to build you and your personal brand from the inside out. It will change your life.

"I knew you before I formed you in your mother's womb. Before you were born I set you apart and appointed you as my prophet to the nations."
Jeremiah 1:5

Chapter 1

Know Yourself

How well do you know yourself? Most people don't know themselves as well as they think they do. Some have lost themselves along the way. They stopped dreaming.

In our society, people who spend too much time thinking about themselves are considered narcissistic. That's because they are. They are usually insecure people hungering for validation.

After all, the great irony of true happiness is not *what can I get for me*? But rather, it's what can I do for others? Adding value to others is what makes you valuable. People will eventually seek you.

High school and/or college is usually when the road to career and self-discovery begins. It's a road worth taking as many miserable people did not seek or find themselves during this time of self-reflection. Their misery has only caused other people pain and suffering. People who have a sense of fulfillment and purpose bring peace into the lives of others.

Life ahead may seem daunting, but don't dismay. Your twenties is the time to find out what you want in life. Discover who you are and why you are here. Each decade brings more clarity. But don't wait too long. It's never too early to get started and never too late to start over. Start now.

Learning how to find your place in life without constantly imposing your frustrations on others is imperative. After all, they are working it out also. If you try to skip this step, you will inevitably come back to this point again. Get comfortable with getting in tune with yourself. No one can help you if you cannot identify the problem yourself. If you are not comfortable with your life or current status, it's time for a change. Change is an opportunity to grow.

If you learn how to do this properly now, you won't have any problems recognizing when it's time to adjust your sails again as you get older. Get used to it. Change is part of life.

Contrary to what some may think, it's not a competition. Your friends have goals also. Each of you has a unique gift or talent. It's a role only you can fill in this world.

Word to the wise [and not so wise], your desires and goals will change. If you have the same desires in your fifties as you did, in your twenties, note to self, you have not grown. You may have the same passions, which is known as your gifts and talents, but you should be expressing them in a more mature, evolved manner as you get older.

When you were hungry as a child, you cried. Others fed you. As an adult, you now make your own meal, request your meal, buy your meal, or pay your personal chef to cater your meal. You know how to get it. Get it?

The primary key is you must first be in tune with what you want. Then go about the most productive and satisfying way for you to attain your desire without imposing on others' rights or personal space. This cannot be over emphasized.

If others have what you need, then recognize their value and compensate them based upon a mutually agreed upon price. It doesn't have to be money. You can barter.

That's what makes the world so beautiful. We need each other. You have what others need and others have what you need. Together, we can help keep the world balanced as it goes around.

Just be considerate and recognize the world doesn't owe you anything. Be grateful for those willing to help you meet your needs even if it's their job to do so. They'll be more willing to help you the next time should you need assistance again.

"The greatest among you shall be your servant" Matthew 23:11

Chapter 2

Your Best Attributes

What are your best attributes? Take a moment to reflect on this. Look at yourself from head to toe, inside and out. What are your best physical, mental, and spiritual qualities?

I once asked this of my five year old niece, and she told me her best attribute was her brain. I was astounded. Was there anything else to say after that? I don't think so. Her answer verified itself. People ten times her age rarely answer as wisely. I think she's going to be okay.

So what are they for you? Many people focus on the aspects of themselves that are not so pleasing to them. I recommend you do the opposite. Start with what you like about yourself.

Physical:

What parts of your body do you like? Is it your eyes, your long fingers, your legs, toes or feet? This may seem like a silly exercise at first, but many people – especially – women – spend a lot of time telling themselves and others what they don't like about themselves.

Most women think they are too fat and most men think their feet smell just fine. Neither is one hundred percent correct. How can anyone else appreciate you if you don't first love, respect, and appreciate your own value?

I remember hearing the story about the man who didn't like his feet. He complained about it all the time until he met the man who had no legs. Don't wait for something extreme to happen for you to be grateful for what God has given you.

If you feel indifferent about this, first start out by expressing gratitude for the parts of your body that work. As you get older you will appreciate the value of this exercise.

We've all heard about people needing new body parts like a kidney, heart, hips, knees, or liver. What they don't realize is the entire body is alive and has memory.

So as you are grumbling about the working body parts you have, you are not exactly watering your personal flower garden. In fact, you are destroying it.

So, look in the mirror. Start giving thanks for your body parts that work. Thank God for it. Do this daily. Watch how what you already have responds better. The body is alive.

Now that you see and appreciate your body's value, take good care of it. Many people take better care of their cars than they do their bodies.

Exercise and nourishing food can turn an okay body into a finely tuned instrument of nature. Now, let's go deeper. How do you see yourself on the inside?

Mental:

Are you balanced? Are you patient? Do you remain calm in chaotic conditions? Are you persistent? Are you an "overcomer"? Do you see the goal rather than the obstacles or do you only tend to see the problems? What are your best mental attributes?

The human mind needs time to focus and time to play. It needs fresh air. It needs to see beauty. It needs to feel appreciated. But you need to be aware of what you feed it.

On the subconscious level, it's always saying yes. It's not like your conscious mind which chooses what you will or won't eat or what you will or will not wear.

The subconscious mind just takes information and absorbs it. It stores it up for later when needed. Advertisers know it. Advertisers know that if they tell you some nonsensical information enough times, you will respond as they indicated when you see their product at some point.

\

Take a look in your closet, garage or kitchen or that of your parents. Is it filled with items you and they don't need, use, or desire?

You need to program yourself consciously for the positive things you want out of life. Otherwise, advertisers and unscrupulous manipulative people will do it for you.

Start by paying attention to the lyrics of any new song before you start repeating it. Decide whether or not it agrees with the direction you want your **personal brand** [your life] to take.

Take a moment to think about the message in a television series before you commit to watching the program regularly. That's why they call it a "program". It's programming you.

Do you like happy and romantic stories? Then you'll likely attract happy and romantic relationships. Do you prefer horror stories and vampires? You'll likely attract a lot of drama into your life and horrible relationships.

It all seems rather silly until years later when you're reminded of it in a relationship, marriage(s), work environment, or event that doesn't seem like you. It is. You just didn't program it consciously. But as long as you're alive and aware, you can change it.

You have a variety of technological options available to you and being offered to you on a daily basis. Decide how you want to use it or how you want to be used by it.

Technology is still fairly new, so people are a bit obsessed with it. Face it. People like new things. However, technology and all its genius and potential thereof cannot replace the human brain. It's so sophisticated, even the best neurologists cannot yet fully explain how the human mind works.

The human brain needs quality food to perform at its best. Quality foods [information and nutrition] are very important.

The brain works best with food from nature. Your mind drinks in the colors: greens, reds, oranges, purples, and yellows and responds in various ways. Colors stimulate different parts of the brain. The nutrition it gets from various colored foods further develops it in areas needed. Red increases blood pressure. Blue lowers blood pressure. Green is good for the heart. Yellow stimulates the brain.

You need a balance of colorful garden grown foods, fish, and water to think properly. Think of the largest creatures that walk the earth, like elephants and giraffes. They are vegetarians.

Humanity is the most sophisticated living creature on the earth. You'd think we'd at least know what to feed ourselves to sustain optimal health [physically, mentally, and spiritually].

I'm not suggesting you become a vegetarian. Just be mindful of the quality of foods you eat. Anything with an extensive shelf life is not going to add value to your life.

People who eat foods loaded with artificial additives and beverages drenched in sugar tend to have difficulty staying focused. Things like attention deficit disorder were not so common in yester years when all foods were grown from the earth and brought to the table.

As a developed society, we should reconsider supplementing poor diet and lack of exercise with pills. Taking chemical substances to stay focused, lose weight, sleep and calm children [and adults] takes its toll on the natural body over time.

When you value your brain, as my niece does, you will find colorful natural garden grown foods you like. Nature has its own code. For example, red and purple foods are often good for the blood. Look at the shape of a walnut. Remind you of anything? It's good snack food for the brain.

You may not like the healthy foods your parents put on your plate and forced you to eat but take the time to try new foods in the vegetable section. Keep going until you find ones you like. Prepare it in different ways, raw, grilled or steamed. Rotate them into your daily food menu.

When you find something's missing or you're feeling blah in some way, research what natural foods benefit that area. It may be as easy as steaming broccoli or learning to love fresh spinach. Experiment with seasonings.

Never underestimate the cliché, *an apple a day keeps the doctor away.* Eating an entire apple, including the seeds, has excellent antioxidant qualities. It builds the immune system.

If you can afford it, get a juicer. Blend fresh fruit and vegetables whole. It's delicious. Trust me. I was a naysayer. Now I treat my juicer like high end furniture. I'm not kidding.

If you're concerned about the shelf life of live foods, select frozen fruits and vegetables. They are frozen at harvest and retain their nutritional value. But fresh is best. Avoid canned fruits and vegetables since preservatives are added.

Since the body is over seventy percent water, guess what you should drink daily? If you guessed water, you're right. Water is like the liquid conductor that keeps everything flowing.

You can't see oxygen, but you know you need it. Water seems so plain and simple, but you can't live without it. Make friends with water. Learn how to swim in it, bathe in it, and drink it. It's everywhere. We need fresh clean water to live.

Everything you need to live well is right inside of you. You just may not have known it.

Spiritual:

This is where it gets icky for some people. Like water and oxygen, many people don't see it, so they think they don't need it. Yet, it's more important than the physical.

It connects where we come from before we are born and where we go to after we die. Yet, there are as many opinions and views on it as the stars in the sky.

It's the one area society agrees on least, and needs the most. So we'll take chapter three to discuss it in detail.

"This is the covenant I will make with the people of Israel after that time," declares the LORD. "I will put my law in their minds and write it on their hearts. I will be their God, and they will be my people." Jeremiah 31:33

Chapter 3

Your Spiritual Life in Focus

No matter who you are, no matter where you are from, no matter what you believe, you have a spiritual identity. In the physical, you have a unique fingerprint unlike any other person in the world. Even twins have different fingerprints and footprints. What's your spiritual identity?

Your soul identity is what you believe in your mind and heart. Your spiritual identity is how God sees you. In God's eyes, He made you perfect. You were created in His [male or female] image. You connect with God and He with you through prayer and meditation.

Beauty, good music and uplifting books feed your soul. What you consistently feed your mind, eventually manifests in your life. The Holy Bible is considered to be soul food but it's really spiritual food as it speaks to the spirit of man.

Many people read it but do not realize it's something to take in small parts and meditate upon just as you would consume a meal. The mind reads the words, but the spirit of man interprets at another level.

Prayer and meditation on the Word of God have changed lives for centuries. People who learn to do this are "checking in" with their Creator to align with their goals and purpose.

If you purchased a high end item that broke, you would call the customer help line. God is the best customer service contact you'll ever know. Even better, it's a toll free call and He's available twenty four hours a day, seven days a week. No budget or travel is required.

People who pray and meditate don't get their answers on a physical level. They get their answer or guidance intuitively.

No one can talk you out of what you know because it's specifically designed for you. You've heard the expression, you know what you know what you know. Well, there comes a point where you just know. You can't explain it. It's like when you've met the person you're going to marry or you've changed careers and no one else understands it. You just found your place. There's peace.

Some people have even heard the audible voice of God. You know it when you hear it. It's like a voice beaming out of your center. Like a parent calling you. No one can deny when he hears his parent's voice.

You'll know God's voice when you hear it. It's always helpful. It will guide you and uplift you. It's never demeaning. The answer always brings peace. Even if you're in danger, He's always calm. After all, who better to change the situation or guide you through it than the Creator of the entire Universe? You just know you're covered.

“Whether you turn to the right or to the left, your ears will hear a voice behind you, saying, "This is the way; walk in it." Isaiah 30:21

Rather than going to psychics and prophets, learn to develop this personal guidance system for yourself. Your Creator designed you with all the information you need inside of you to succeed in whatever you were sent to the world to share.

No one will [or should] be more interested in your purpose than you. Your pastor can help develop and guide you, but ultimately you need to learn how to feed yourself spiritually.

You feed your body daily. Feed your soul and spirit daily too. It's the part that governs the mind and its direction.

Start your day in prayer and meditation. Even if it's only five or ten minutes as a daily morning habit, you will see the difference. It preps your day. It's powerful.

If you can, start your day reading a chapter or verse in the Holy Bible. Listen to a faith filled inspirational audio CD on your way to class or to work. Get daily inspirational text messages from a pastor you respect and enjoy. Watch a daily message from the archives on their website or on YouTube.

It's spiritual food. Eat daily. All of this may sound hokey until you start seeing changes for the better in your life.

When you're looking for yourself and desire to know who you are and why you are here, you want real answers. When you are young, it's normal. When people go down the wrong road, some find themselves trying to fill the emptiness they often find with drugs, sex and alcohol. Yet, they are never satisfied.

It's like stuffing yourself with a box of donuts. It starts off tasting really good. Then, you get a stomach ache and cavities. Guess what? You're still hungry. There is no physical, mental, or spiritual nutritional value in it. It's garbage.

So what's the answer? It may sound too easy, but the truth often is. You must seek your manufacturer [your Creator a.k.a. God] to understand why you were made [sent].

It's easy. Close your eyes. Take a deep breath. Now, ask God for your true purpose. Wait for the answer.

Be prepared. He'll answer in a way only you could understand. Keep your eyes and ears open over the next few days, weeks, months ahead as the answer unfolds tailor made just for you.

Dr. Myles Munroe describes in beautiful detail the five attributes everyone must know to live a fulfilling life. I shared these attributes briefly in my previous book, ***The Answer Key to Avoid Debt, Build Credit & Retire Rich,*** but I believe it is better suited here since we are developing your personal brand. Take a moment to ask and answer these questions for yourself.

1) **Who Am I**? – Getting to know yourself as we mentioned is the first step. Who are your parents? What is their culture? Where were you born? What beliefs did they share with you that you carry on today? Ethnicity is a PLUS. Today's society requires you to be aware of other cultures. If you or your parents are bilingual or multi-lingual, say so. Show it in your blog, video, or social media profile. This increases your marketability and value to multinational corporations. Today, the internet forces all companies to be multi-cultural on some level. After all, the internet is international.

2) **Where am I from?** – Are you from a big town, small town, urban or suburban environment? More importantly and deeper than that, what is your Source? Who is your God? Who sent you to your parents and why?

3) **Why am I here?** When you get to the root of your Source – your God – you can then ask properly the reason why you were sent into this world. What is your true purpose?

4) **What can you do**? What are your natural gifts and talents? What comes easily to you? How can you share it to benefit others?

5) **Where am I going?** What is your destiny? Do you know it? Don't just drift or worse let others decide for you. Get in alignment with your destiny. Get in touch with your Source and discover your purpose and your destiny.

Some of you may be thinking, this doesn't sound very spiritual. I can assure you it is.

Our perception of "spiritual" is often muddled due to centuries of other people's interpretations. However, the ultimate key is your own personal relationship with God which can be acquired through personal prayer and meditation and reading the Bible for yourself.

No one should be more interested in your personal growth and development than you. Don't put the responsibility on your parents, mentors, teachers and pastors alone. Take responsibility for yourself. After all, you are the one person that will be with you one hundred percent of the time for the rest of your life.

Only God can be with you twenty four hours a day, seven days a week. Get to know Him. You would be surprised what He knows about you. I have found that no matter how high my goals, God's plans are bigger and He always does better.

You'll find most people who are extremely successful take time to pray and meditate in some way. Some call it focus.

Meditation is more. It's like having the answers to the exam in advance. Life is often referred to as an open book test. But most people don't take time to open the book [Bible] or get to know themselves. Today's your lucky day. Get started.

Chapter 4

On the Job Experience

Society has changed so much. Finding a job or starting a career has almost changed entirely since your parents graduated from high school or college. Many people work from home on their computers. Others just check into the office a few times each week.

Your parents had the experience of working alongside others. Networking was easy. Right associations can help build character.

Working with others develops you in ways you could never accomplish on your own. Assuming you are working in a field you enjoy, you will likely find people with mutual interests. Many times you have different strengths. Perhaps each of you completes a different portion of a project.

Finding an internship or a job in a field you may pursue in a career later is extremely important. If you can manage to do this while you are still in high school or college, find a quality employer [small or large] where you can get a taste of the potential career [industry or field].

The field of interest and the professionalism of the people therein are the only things that matter. Don't be overly concerned about the salary right now. You need experience. Your salary will [*should*] rise with your value.

If it's an environment that can truly help you learn, work for free as an intern if you must. Just get your foot in the door. Nothing's worse than pursuing a degree in a career you think you'll love, only to find out on your first post graduation job that you hate it.

Since more people are now working from home, you can find out if you work better as a team or alone. You need to know that early. Are you disciplined enough to work on your own or are you better with a definitive schedule and guidance from a manager? Some people get motivated by daily association with their peers.

Potential employers and their staff often feel less threatened by an intern making copies or getting coffee. You can learn a lot if you keep your eyes and ears open.

You may even get lucky. It may be an environment you'd like to work in after you graduate. You've already proven that you are assertive and self-motivated. This may be a future employer or at least a referral.

Either way, you win. You are building your personal brand and your resume.

If you're someone who is seeking a new job or career, this works too. If you've been unemployed awhile, contact your ideal employer[s] and offer to work with them for a month for free. They get to see your value. **Do your very best.**

Ask for a personal evaluation with management at the end of the month. Many people have gotten their ideal job and salary this way.

Extra Bonus:

Find a local non-profit organization where you can volunteer your time and/or donate to at least once per month. It should be in alignment with your goals and/or values.

This not only adds tremendous value to your character, but many employers use this as a deciding factor between final candidates. It is used again when considering promotions. It shows initiative and is a positive reflection on the company and you.

Chapter 5

Priceless Intangible Assets

"Do you not know that you are the Temple of God, and that The Spirit of God dwells within you?" 1 Corinthians 3:16

Before we delve further into the tangle assets as education, personal skills, and work experience, let's talk about your intangible assets. What are they?

Trustworthy: Can you be trusted with personal information? Do you repeat a secret after a friend or associate has confided in you? Do you read other's mail, email when they are not looking? Can you be trusted not to divulge personal or confidential information provided to you through an individual or company.

Reliable: Do you show up on time? Do you do what you say you will do?

Loyal: Do you talk about others behind their backs? Do you job hunt online while at work? Do you speak negatively about your peers, work associates, previous employers, or clients when they are not there or when being interviewed?

Honest: Do you tell the truth even when it is inconvenient or unpopular to do so?

Integrity: Do you still behave honestly and do the right thing even when others are not looking? Do you do the right thing when given the opportunity to take a short cut or undermine others?

Morals and Values: The basic premise is the Golden Rule: *Do unto others as you would have them do unto you.* You respect all your customers, peers and employees. You maintain a high level of excellence. You respect yourself and others in a way that those who follow will recognize as the highest standard.

Discerning: Having the wisdom to know the difference between right and wrong. If you lack it, read **Book of Proverbs**. [*Available at our website*]

Quality: Go beyond the minimum requirements. Go the extra mile. People who do so are continuously setting themselves up for promotion, pay increase, referrals, and steady clients.

Dependable: Do you do what you say you will do consistently? Can people trust you to complete a project on time?

Over time, these assets can become more valuable than the tangible assets. People can be trained to do a job or build a career or talent. However, the above characteristics are the crown jewels of long term success that help create a lasting legacy for others to follow. Ultimately, most people want to have the above said about them by their children and successors.

Whenever possible, find employers that share your values or surpass yours. That way, you are always moving upward and forward amicably.

Chapter 6

Your Social Profile

Coming from a generation that only had three major tv channels, landlines, and pay phones, I have mixed feelings about social media. I've seen it operate at its best and worse.

On the one hand it's wonderful to have access to information at the click of a button. On the other hand, this is the first generation that may pay the price for just being a kid if they are not aware of the long term implications of their social media posts today. There are some unscrupulous people, companies, and organizations out there hacking into people's private phones, computers, and cable boxes to see what they are saying and doing. That's not okay.

Previous generations could just tell silly jokes and not have it played back to them twenty years later. They could party, make silly faces and wear clothes any way they wanted to express their personalities without having it played back to them when they pursued a high profile job position as President or CEO as an adult thirty years later.

Personally, I enjoy reading posts and seeing and sharing pictures with family and friends from high school or college. Most of them are just as funny as they were then.

I truly enjoy hearing about others success, travels, and experiences. Ideally, one should have a safe haven to share these intimate details and updates with friends and loved ones at the click of a button.

Social media facilitates our ability to catch up things. We share wedding announcements, birth of a child, events, personal progress or setbacks as well as recent pictures of our new friends, peers, family etc. Many receive leads for a new job or position. Sometimes it's just a word of encouragement. In this way, social media can be priceless.

However, when one of us is being considered for a high profile position, we're all being interviewed so to speak. That's not always so fun. So choose your friends and posts wisely.

That said, you should be aware that anything you say or do in social media today can be used against you or for you later. Everything on the internet is archived somewhere.

You almost have to live as if you will be president one day. Perhaps you need to create a public and private profile.

One would like to think you can have a private conversation with friends and family without it being repeated. Just be sure you know who your "friends" are. If they are questionable and you are sharing something somewhat revealing, post it privately.

Private conversations now require friends and family turn off their cellular phones. First, it should be out of respect for giving one's full attention to the conversation. It's also good etiquette. That good etiquette requirement can also prevent others from recording the entire conversation for playback later.

Be honest with yourself about family members who think you are either high and mighty or a loser. You'll know this because family usually has no problem telling you. Don't use them as a referral. Sound too obvious? You'd be surprised.

The same goes with anyone you are dating. If you're not married, don't allow anyone to take nude pictures or video of you no matter how tempting. The relationship may be going great today, but once people break up you'd be amazed at how vengeful some people can be. Don't do it. You won't have any regrets later.

Believe it or not, many people today are hired or fired based upon their Twitter, Facebook, LinkedIn, YouTube or Instagram feeds. Some very high security places will even ask for your password [illegal in some states] to see what you and others have written, review your internet browsing habits, email and check your telephone records. Many employers will just ask to "friend" you on Facebook, Twitter, Instagram etc to view your activities. You are not obligated to accept or approve.

Are you calling your bookie, drug dealer, or searching porn? Does this all sound too personal? It is.

All of this affects the way you make decisions on the job. But I agree. I believe there is a better way to do this.

Like I said, technology is still new, and man still has not figured out how the human mind works entirely. If they did, they would know that respect of another human life in the highest regard is the way to get the best out of people.

I'm just sharing the facts. I hope it will better prepare you. I've seen social media "profiling" done to others – including myself.

Privacy laws have not quite caught up with technology, but needs to. This book is just to prepare you for what is taking place in many high profile jobs for which most people are completely unprepared. Perhaps you or one of your peers will be the one to get personal rights and privacy laws in place to protect you and others during the speedy ascent of technology.

Don't let any of this deter you from aspiring to high profile positions. Pursue them fervently. Just have the knowledge you need to transcend any obstacles or to change current laws to meet consumer needs. After all, there is always room at the top for people with integrity.

With the knowledge you gain in this book, the value of your personal brand will surely multiply. Shine on. We need it. That's why you're here.

Chapter 7

Credit Profile

Most people don't think about their credit until they apply for an apartment, home mortgage or car loan. But you do need to know your credit score.

Not only do you need it to get approved for an apartment in a good location, a home or a car, but many employers now review your credit report to see how responsible you are. Do you pay your bills? If so, do you pay them on time? Do you dodge your creditors? Are you honest? How many times have you moved in the last two years? All of this can be seen in your credit report.

Initially, you won't have any credit. So you will need to build it. Read **The Answer Key to Avoid Debt, Build Credit & Retire Rich.** It will show you how to consciously build your credit. Do this before you get a credit card or especially if you already have one.

Once you get your credit established, request your annual credit report. You get one copy free every year [via Equifax, Experian, and Transunion in USA only]. Your actual credit score is provided for a small additional fee.

Make sure there are no errors in your credit report. Correct errors immediately if you find any. Update them with your current address.

Good credit can put you leaps ahead of others who may even be making more than you and graduated with top honors. Develop good credit early and keep it. You'll never regret it.

Chapter 8

Get Paid to Polish your Skills

This is something that is very easy to do. It will not only set you apart from the competition, it will show you have drive and initiative. You'll also be building your resume and meeting potential employers.

One of the major advantages of growing up with technology is that many of you have some serious computer skills. Put your experience to good use and get paid.

Many startups today are looking for every day people with a few good skills. Are you an artist? You can design logos or design websites or product packages via 99designs.com. Artists place bids [cost of doing the work] on upcoming jobs. If your bid and timeframe is accepted, you get the job. Work from home, campus, or your dorm. Complete the assignment and get paid. It's a great way to build your resume and referrals.

Do you design software or hardware programs? Are you a good writer? Like to blog? Some companies will even hire you to update their Facebook and Twitter feeds.

Check out elance.com or Freelancer.com. Find jobs that you can complete with the highest degree of integrity. Don't bid on all of them. Just the ones you know you can do well.

Remember, you are building the personal brand of Y-O-U! Make it stand out with the quality of your work. Go the extra mile. Give exceptional service. Deliver on time.

Many companies hire the same quality people consistently on a freelance basis. You're building your resume, and meeting potential long term employers. It's a great way to make additional income while in college, after college, or between jobs. Some people leave full time employment, and work when they want via these freelance jobs. It's good to have choices.

If it's a startup company, you may be one of the initial employees. That's what happened at Google, Microsoft, Apple, Facebook, and many others. It made millionaires and billionaires out of many of its initial employees and steady freelancers.

If you have a unique, yet kosher, perspective and others listen to your opinions, share it in a blog [Wordpress, Blogger etc.] or video blog [i.e. YouTube channel or Vimeo] Many fashionistas, musicians, writers, performers are now starting their careers here and getting international coverage. It's hard to say what blog or video will go viral today. Just be honest and original. It should also go without saying, but be well groomed and sober.

Chapter 9

Find a Mentor

A good mentor can guide you around and over the obstacles and safely land you where you wish to be. It can save you a lot of time just as this book will for many.

What makes a good mentor?

Someone who you respect for his or her accomplishments, honesty, success and/or integrity in life or in a particular field/industry is a good mentor. This person does not have to be high profile. It can be a parent, aunt, uncle, relative, coach, guidance counselor, or teacher. They recognize your potential. They believe in you. You want someone who encourages you and who will push you to be your very best.

You can find mentors through business networks or social groups you join [i.e. SCORE.org, MicroMentor.org, or MeetUp.com]. It can be a manager, current or retired entrepreneur or executive, team leader, personal coach or motivational speaker.

Choose someone who will tell you the truth when others won't or don't. The higher you get in status or position, the more difficult this can be.

Be able to discern constructive criticism. Don't choose someone who belittles you. Your mentor should be a good listener, and yet you should be doing most of the listening.

Be clear about what you want. Take one to three items that you are working on to discuss with him or her. Don't take up too much of their time. After all, you want to be able to sit and speak with them again.

Offer to take that person out for coffee, tea, or lunch at your expense and within your budget. Just make sure it's a nice clean environment and someplace where you can hear each other speak. There are many nice cafes these days. Choose one.

If your parents are members of a country club or someplace nice, choose that. It doesn't take a lot of money. Just be considerate of their time and make sure you show up on time to your appointment. Get there before him or her.

Initially, you may not be able to afford a personal coach or advisor but you should never be the one always on the take. What can you give that person?

If you can't afford to pay for a cup of coffee, snack, or lunch, offer to do extra chores for your parent or coach. Perhaps you can assist him or her at a seminar or running errands.

Never accept or offer to do sexual favors or purchase drugs or illicit material. *Is she really saying that?* Yes, I am. If I am saying it, it's because it happens to some people. The answer is always no. Find another mentor.

Get in the habit of looking out for those who help you succeed. Make it a lifetime habit. It will serve you well.

Even if it's your personal assistant and you already pay him or her. Especially, if it's your assistant or an employee and that person is exceptional, be kind.

Be sure that you give them every reason to speak with you again with honesty and integrity. You can't pay someone to be loyal, but if you pay them well, you will show them your gratitude which often brings loyalty in return.

If you do not know anyone who can mentor you in your desired field, go to the Small Business Association [SBA.com]. Many services are free. You'll also find some workshops with small fees that can further you along.

The mentors at SCORE are volunteers. Many are retired executives or entrepreneurs willing to share their experiences and insight. Call to schedule an appointment to meet in person. Ask to meet with someone in your industry whenever possible.

You can expand your options by going to their website, SCORE.org. Schedule a telephone or Skype appointment with a mentor in another city who is more closely associated and experienced in your desired field. If you meet in person, be sure it's at the organization's office or in a public place. Show up on time. Schedule a follow up appointment. Be accountable.

Chapter 10

Planning Your Future

Now, people often think I mean planning for the future. That's what we did in all the previous chapters. This chapter is different. This is a personal written exercise. It has literally changed the course of many people's lives. Perhaps it will do the same for you, especially if you were headed in the wrong direction. This will help get you on a better path.

Get a brand new notebook for this. This is a notebook you may have for at least forty years. I'm not kidding. I can't even describe how people respond to this. I've seen tears and relationship reconciliations. You name it. You have no idea.

Let's get started. First sit back and relax. I want you to now think about your future. Picture yourself as an older person. Let's say sixty – eighty – ninety – or even one hundred years old. Imagine you are telling someone, perhaps your grandchildren or great grandchildren, about your life.

Before we continue, I must warn you that the majority of the people, if not all- actually get what they project. So I highly recommend you do this alone and do not be silly or angry at anyone when you do this. Any ill will to others will not accomplish anything good for you.

Do not name other people you want to see in this picture. You can describe them as a spouse or your children etc, but you don't get to choose other people's future. They will only resent you for it [intuitively]. If you are already happily married and have children, then of course you can include them.

So please, please, please make up a wonderful story with great relationships, wonderful people, good health, super actions and doing, loving, and living way beyond your current level of life. Get that warm fuzzy feeling inside when you tell how spectacular your life has been.

Write it down in your notebook in the past tense as if it has already happened. Read it aloud to yourself. Close the book.

"And the LORD answered me, and said, 'Write the vision, and make it plain upon tables, that he may run that readeth it.'" Habakkuk 2:2

I really don't have more to say about this except, you'll likely start noticing people, places, and opportunities start coming into alignment with this long term image. If life ever starts to become unbearable, sit down and reimage the ending.

Remember the Golden Rule. *Do unto other as you would have them do unto you.* It's as simple and accurate as H2O.

"The most important one," answered Jesus, "is this: 'Hear, O Israel: The Lord our God, the Lord is one. Love the Lord your God with all your heart and with all your soul and with all your mind and with all your strength.' The second is this: 'Love your neighbor as yourself.' There is no commandment greater than these." Mark 12:29-31

Chapter 11

Be You

Many of us admire people in our youth only to find out later, they aren't necessarily who we thought they were. But that's life. Many people have a personal face with friends and family and a public face which is how they want to be perceived.

As you grow, and come into alignment with the person God created you to be, you will become more comfortable in your own skin. Some of you will discover your gifts and talents early. It makes some people seem quirky. Just give it time. It will all make sense later.

Get comfortable with your originality as you present your gifts to the world. Sometimes being "different" makes people feel out of place. But often times, these are the pioneers of our society. With the right intent, it brings progress. Hopefully, you will discover the grace in your gift and honor the world with your offerings. **Remember, it's what you give to the world that determines your value**. If it's good, don't hold back. Share it.

Ultimately, you will not be completely happy imitating others. So get busy. Discover who you are and why you are here. You're the answer to someone else's problem. Discover it.

I can assure you, it's always better than you think. It will bring great joy, relief and peace to others. You will be rewarded for sharing it. Package it the best way you can and slap a price tag on it. The bigger the problem your gift solves for others, the more you can charge to provide the solution. It will be worth it. If you can package it and provide it at a lower price in mass quantities, you can receive perpetual income for life.

Just do us all a favor, be you. No one else can fill your shoes. No one else can be you.

Recognize your value. Put your best foot forward. The world is waiting for the authentic God sent you. So show up.

"For I know the plans I have for you," says the LORD. "They are plans for good and not for disaster, to give you a future and a hope." Jeremiah 29:11

You may also enjoy the original DVD from which this book is written, **Developing Your #1 Brand, YOU!** *[Live Speech to students at Nazareth College]* and **The Book of Proverbs Journal**. Find both [and lots more] at our website. Enjoy!

<u>SoRichIam.com</u>